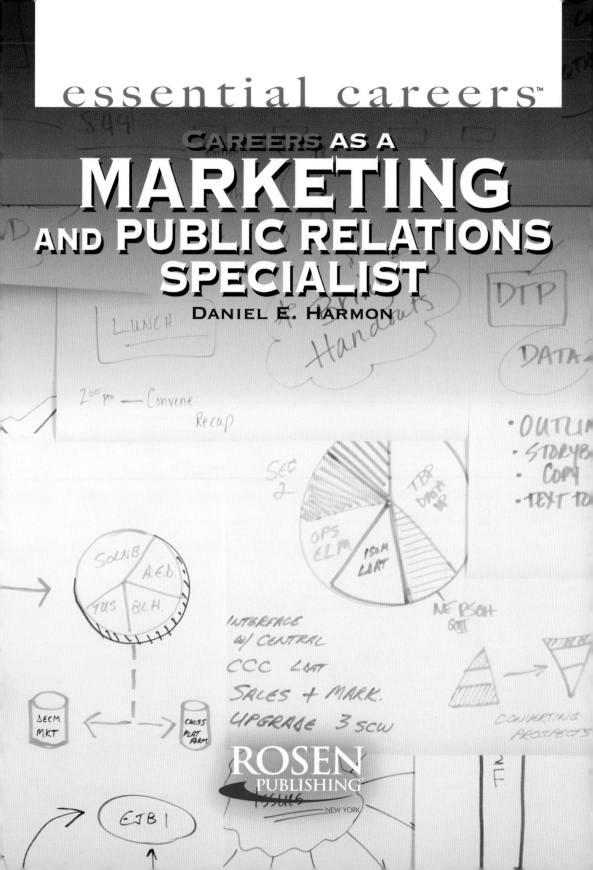

essential careers™

CAREERS AS A
MARKETING
AND PUBLIC RELATIONS
SPECIALIST

DANIEL E. HARMON

ROSEN
PUBLISHING

NEW YORK

Published in 2014 by The Rosen Publishing Group, Inc.
29 East 21st Street, New York, NY 10010

Library of Congress Cataloging-in-Publication Data

Harmon, Daniel E.
Careers as a marketing and public relations specialist/Daniel E. Harmon.
     pages cm. — (Essential careers)
Includes bibliographical references and index.
ISBN 978-1-4777-1793-6 (library binding)
1. Marketing—Vocational guidance. 2. Public relations—Vocational guidance. I. Title.
HF5415.35.H37 2014
658.0023—dc23

                                                                2013016223

Manufactured in Malaysia

CPSIA Compliance Information: Batch #W14YA: For further information, contact Rosen Publishing, New York, New York, at 1-800-237-9932.

contents

INTRO

Marketing and PR teams meet regularly to share and discuss creative ideas, strategies, and assignments. Teams in large firms typically include professionals with different skills.

DUCTION

The famous old saying may be more accurate today than ever before: "It pays to advertise." That's because competition is fierce and becoming fiercer.

In horse-and-buggy times, if you owned the only grocery store or bank in town and the next town was 30 miles (48 kilometers) away, there was little need to promote your business. Local customers had no other place to go. Now consumers everywhere have many choices. They look for the best products and services at the lowest prices. If they don't like any of the selections available in their city or neighborhood, they look online. A seller located 1,000 miles (1,609 km) away might offer just what they need at a bargain price. Next-day delivery is usually inexpensive.

Marketing, public relations (PR), and advertising will always be vital in free enterprise societies. As long as there is marketplace competition, competitors must persuade customers to buy from them. Marketing and PR professionals are trained to effectively communicate a seller's message to a buying public.

Historians suggest that certain paintings in prehistoric caves might be considered primitive advertisements in a way. They told of hunting prowess, for example, and depicted symbols of wealth. Mark Tungate, in *Ad Land: A Global History of Advertising*, says, "It's safe to say that advertising has been around for as long as there have been goods to sell and a medium to talk them up—from the crier in the street to the handbill tacked to a tree."

Some businesses do their own promotion. In the twenty-first century, though, competition has become increasingly intense and complex. Business owners rely on knowledgeable and experienced marketing and PR professionals to help ensure success.

Dozens of specific jobs are part of the marketing and PR professions. The International Association of Business Communicators includes members who work in separate but often related roles. They include community relations, public and media relations, government relations, investor relations, corporate communications, marketing communications, public affairs, advertising, writing, editing, training and teaching, photography and video production, graphic design, and human resources.

Who hires these professionals? Clients include major national and international corporations: car manufacturers, airlines, grocery and restaurant chains, and makers of all sorts of consumer products. Entertainment agents and publicists represent music and film celebrities as well as little-known performers. Some marketing specialists are in the thick of political campaigns; they generate positive publicity for candidates and shape campaign platforms and strategies.

Most marketing and PR firms and individuals, however, serve local and regional clients. They publicize area businesses. Some serve as spokespersons for organizations and government agencies. They help their clients educate the public on a variety of topics, from personal finances to legal concerns to physical fitness.

Marketing specialists don't exist merely to make money for their clients. In the end, they serve society. They provide useful information to help consumers make smart buying decisions and lifestyle choices.

Marketing and public relations present young people with exciting, diverse career opportunities to consider. The future of the professions is bright.

chapter 1

MARKETING

Marketing and public relations are related but different. Basically, marketing is the promotion and advertising of a business, product, or service. Public relations, or PR, is the ongoing process of informing the public about the doings of the client, using different news media.

In large marketing and advertising firms, PR is usually one of many services they provide for clients. Professionals in this area may perform public relations as well as other marketing tasks. Specialists may focus on just one role or several.

Some marketing and PR professionals work in agencies that are hired by clients. Their clients may include individuals, large manufacturing and retail corporations, small businesses, organizations, and government departments or offices. Other professionals are employed by a particular industry or organization. Employers include professional, educational, scientific, technical, manufacturing, financial, and insurance companies and institutions.

WHAT DO MARKETING PROFESSIONALS DO?

Enterprises and organizations hire marketers to develop elaborate, ongoing promotional campaigns. Marketing professionals think of their work as something of a science.

Here are some of the services that marketing firms provide for their clients:

MARKET RESEARCH AND ANALYSIS

Marketers carefully examine sales statistics and trends. They learn which types of consumers (young or old, male or female, etc.) are most likely to buy the client's products. This information helps them focus their advertising budgets on the most promising consumer groups.

PLANNING A MARKETING CAMPAIGN

Planners decide which forms of advertising and promotion will most likely be effective in creating interest in the client's

Like this shoe shopper, all consumers are confronted with choices. The marketing professional's task is to make the client's products prominent in the eyes of a targeted buying audience.

products or services. They try to think like the consumers in their target audience. Grocery and home product shoppers, for example, regularly sift through newspaper inserts and mailed circulars. People who spend a lot of time online are most likely to be drawn by Web site and search engine pop-up ads. Planners focus marketing campaigns wherever buyers are likely to be found.

BRANDING AND POSITIONING

Branding is creating an identity for a client company that is instantly recognized by consumers. The company name is one part of its brand. Its distinctive logo is another. The famous Apple logo—an apple that's been bitten into—immediately tells buyers a computer or mobile device is a product of Apple Inc. The bright red Coca-Cola logo, used for many years to identify the soft drink, is easily recognized at a distance.

Other elements of a brand might include a catchy slogan, an unusual color tint or combination, or a shape (such as the unmistakable Coca-Cola bottle and the classic Jeep). In radio and television commercials, a short, memorable jingle that becomes associated with the advertiser in listeners' minds is part of the brand.

Some marketing firms specialize in branding. Much of their work involves rebranding. If a company's popularity and sales are trending downward, the company may change its brand as a way of reinventing and relaunching itself.

Another marketing strategy is positioning. What feature sets a product apart from its competitors? Does it function in a completely different way? Is it intended for a specialty market—a small, concentrated group of customers who have particular needs or interests? Will it be viewed as a budget item or as an expensive, showy selection that's popular among the rich and famous?

Over time, successful branding can make a company and its products instantly recognizable. The Coca-Cola logo and classic bottle shape are familiar even in Vietnam, where this sign is displayed.

PUTTING THE CAMPAIGN PLAN IN ACTION

The scope of marketing campaigns varies. The opening of a new store in town might be trumpeted effectively with newspaper advertisements, press releases, a grand-opening ceremony sponsored by the chamber of commerce, and the circulation of sale flyers. When large corporations want to generate buzz for a new product, service, office expansion, or merger, much of the marketing goes online. That may involve revising or creating new Web pages, Web advertising, e-mailed press announcements to hundreds or thousands of media outlets, and media/public networking. Other marketing tools include direct-mail, print, and online brochures and "sell sheets," and e-newsletters.

Large marketing campaigns call for the skills of a team of marketing agency employees. For certain small, local projects, one professional may be able to perform all the work.

PERFORMING SPECIFIC TASKS

Marketing firms often hire specialists to perform different functions. Employees who have both creative and technical skills design and maintain Web sites for client corporations. Others set up and produce client podcasts, video presentations, and webinars. Webinars are conferences conducted online. The president or a key officer of the client company leads a webinar, interacting with participants in remote locations.

Experienced writers use their talents to write articles for clients' newsletters and blogs. Workers with good PR skills run information booths and make product demonstrations at trade shows and other events. Trained workers conduct telephone and e-mail surveys to measure consumer needs and customer satisfaction.

Advertising departments have their own expert staffs to produce client ads for print, broadcast, and online media. They include copywriters, art and design professionals, and media representatives.

MARKETING MANAGERS

The top jobs in the marketing workforce are at the management level. The U.S. Bureau of Labor Statistics' *Occupational Outlook Handbook* reports that many marketing, advertising, and promotions managers command salaries in six figures. Managers plan and develop a marketing program tailored for a specific client. They work with business clients and with staff personnel, including PR and advertising professionals, sales representatives, art directors, and financial specialists.

Managers discuss with their clients and team members such issues as client contracts, which products should be the focus of a marketing campaign, and

In this graphic design office, artists in a brainstorming session develop visual concepts for a project by viewing an assortment of printed images.

which media will probably be most effective. They identify which groups of consumers are most likely to be interested in a product. Managers also help clients decide on product pricing—pricing that is both affordable for buyers and profitable for the seller.

Managers collect and organize information for planning the campaign. They do not perform specific tasks, such as market research, advertising design, and copywriting, but they oversee those jobs. Managers hire staff members or approve hiring decisions.

While most daily work is performed within the firm, managers frequently go to clients' offices and media headquarters. For major accounts, this may require extensive travel out of town. Managers basically work regular weekday schedules, but overtime is common. The work is usually fast-paced. It can be very stressful and require night and weekend hours as deadlines approach.

The U.S. Bureau of Labor Statistics (BLS) expects the number of marketing management jobs to grow at an annual rate of 14 percent between now and 2020.

RELATED MARKETING JOBS

Marketing firms and corporate marketing departments hire workers who have different types of skills. Here are a few of the related job classifications and specialties:

MARKET RESEARCH ANALYSTS

These professionals study statistics and trends. They carefully examine buying habits over a period of time in a local or broader market area. They try to accurately estimate a product's sales potential. This information helps their employers decide product prices, which media to use for advertising, and other marketing issues.

RUNNING A MARKETING FIRM

Markets constantly change. Marketing organizations change with them. In her career spanning almost twenty years, Amy Juers has transformed from a marketing client to a successful marketer in her own right.

Juers is president of Edge Legal Marketing. Her firm serves a niche market: legal professionals and companies that provide law-related products and services. Based in St. Paul, Minnesota, Edge is a "virtual" operation that serves clients in five countries. Juers and several of her eleven employees live in Minneapolis/St. Paul, but others live and work in different parts of the country. They collaborate online and by phone.

After working as an information specialist for a legal services company, Juers became the company's marketing manager. Her company contracted with a firm called LegalVoice to handle its public relations. In time, Juers went to work for LegalVoice and became its chief executive officer (CEO). Under her guidance, the firm expanded into full-service marketing. Eventually, she transformed it into Edge Legal Marketing.

The biggest challenge of a marketing professional, she says, is keeping everyone focused together. "You often have a lot of people from various departments bringing ideas to the table, and you need to be able to manage expectations and predict outcomes and be confident in your decisions."

Juers says another challenge is demonstrating to skeptical clients the long-term value of public relations.

ART DIRECTORS

Art directors guide the visual features of a marketing plan. They develop the overall look of advertisements, product packaging, and other graphic materials for print media and for television and video productions.

GRAPHIC DESIGNERS

Designers create the advertisements and other visual materials envisioned by their art directors. Some of their work is done by hand, but computer art and design programs have become vital.

Art directors and graphic designers also work in PR firms and departments.

Designers discuss layout elements on a laptop computer. Computer art and design programs have become essential in modern advertising and periodical design work.

TECHNICAL STAFF

These include video specialists who produce broadcast commercials and online presentations. They also include computer specialists who help create and support multimedia presentations and demonstrations.

SALES MANAGERS

Marketing and public relations are not the same as sales. In some large corporations, marketing and PR departments work closely with sales teams. They have different responsibilities, though. The role of marketing and publicity professionals is to draw positive consumer attention to the business and its products. This lays the groundwork for the sales force to succeed. Sales representatives actively sell the products to customers. They answer questions, negotiate discounts, and complete the deal.

Sales managers are in charge of sales teams. They establish goals and monitor sales statistics. They also oversee sales training programs.

PRODUCT DEMONSTRATORS AND PROMOTERS

Demonstrators and promoters show products to consumers in stores, in malls, at public events, and on television. They answer questions and explain their products' benefits and values. Promoters demonstrate a variety of goods, including food, housewares, cosmetics, and apparel.

TELEMARKETERS

The telemarketing business came under heavy criticism in the late 1900s. Citizens were angered by countless telephone calls from agents trying to sell them all kinds of products and services that were of no interest. Despite the government's Do-Not-Call remedy, telemarketing thrives. For young people interested in marketing careers, a stint as a telemarketer can be an instructive experience. (And it will look good on a résumé.)

THE MARKETING-PR CONNECTION

In many agencies and offices, people in this career field perform a variety of related tasks. Marketing often encompasses advertising, public relations, and other methods to promote the client company and its wares.

Usually, professionals focus their careers on either marketing or public relations. PR calls for a particular set of communication skills.

chapter 2

PUBLIC RELATIONS

Public relations professionals have come to be dubbed "spin doctors." Their job is to cast their client companies, organizations, and individuals in the most favorable public light. They generate good press for their clients. They create and keep up positive public images for the people who hire them.

Practically every business and organization needs good public relations. Most small operations cannot afford to hire PR professionals. Whenever they have good news to report—opening a new facility, a state or national award, a special accomplishment—the owner or manager simply phones the local newspaper office or TV station. Larger organizations pay PR workers to generate a regular stream of good publicity. Some have PR specialists or staffs in-house. Others retain a PR agency to handle their public affairs.

PR professionals serve a broad range of businesses and institutions. Clients include major international corporations and small businesses. Hospital, university, and public school systems need public relations specialists. So do government agencies at all levels. Professional firms—law offices, tax preparers, doctors, and dentists, for example—understand the value of public relations and marketing.

Effective PR goes beyond feeding news to the press. It may involve direct interaction with existing and potential customers. For public corporations, it includes a company's relations with its investors.

Public watchdog organizations and media critics regard PR workers with a tinge of suspicion. If a client company or celebrity becomes embroiled in scandal or controversy, it's the PR representative's job to prevent permanent damage to the reputation, if possible. PR agents occasionally have to confront hard-nosed questions from reporters.

Much of the "news" published every day in many papers and magazines around the world is taken from press announcements. This "news" was written and circulated by PR firms. Some of the better-written press releases (the ones containing interesting information, as opposed to advertising fluff) are published word for word.

Jim Macnamara, an Australian professor and author on PR and media topics, conducted a study of press releases in the 1990s. He traced 150 news releases sent out by 27 PR firms. He found that almost a third of them were the bases of

Public relations sometimes requires informing the public about disasters and controversies. Here, military, civilian, and corporate officials meet the press to discuss the 2010 oil spill in the Gulf of Mexico.

published news articles. PR also provides material for broadcast news programs.

News services constantly look for interesting information. If a PR firm can provide them with articles and background information about a client, it may become news. This form of publicity can be far more valuable to the client than paid advertisements.

WHAT DO PUBLIC RELATIONS PROFESSIONALS DO?

Tasks performed by PR firms and specialists include the following:

ESTABLISH MEDIA RELATIONS

Public relations professionals work with members of the media every day. They get to know news and entertainment journalists who might take an interest in their clients' products and activities. Over time, they build relationships of trust. They try to provide information that will be truly useful and interesting to readers and viewers. If they succeed, reporters and editors give special attention to their news releases. Journalists know the material will be worth considering—not thinly veiled advertisements.

PR professionals keep their media contact files up to date. They are always on the lookout for new media professionals to approach.

The White House press secretary conducts news briefings each day on behalf of the president. The media contact answers reporters' questions about various executive policy issues.

ESTABLISH CLIENT RELATIONS

When a PR firm or specialist takes on a new client, the professional becomes thoroughly familiar with the client's products. The representative should learn enough to be able to answer detailed questions if contacted by a reporter.

PR agents are in regular contact with key people in the client organization. They meet to discuss products under development, new services, and fresh publicity angles.

CARRY OUT PR TASKS

PR involves a wide range of activities. Specialists write press releases and distribute them to journalists. News releases announce new products and services. They report details when a client company acquires or merges with another, expands operations, or relocates. Press announcements tell of staff promotions and new hires of special importance. They announce awards and other successes. They also publicize upcoming events in which the client will take part or act as a sponsor.

Writers also engage in long-term projects. They write feature articles, in-depth whitepapers, newsletters, and case studies about a client's activities. They develop press kits and keep them up to date. Press kits are folders or packets of extensive information about the client company, prepared for use by members of the press. A press kit typically contains descriptions of the company's products and services. It provides brief biographies of the executive officers and department heads, contact information, and a history of the company. It may include case studies of how individual customers have benefited from the company's offerings. It presents the company's mission statement and often includes short testimonials from enthusiastic customers.

PR includes broadcast and Internet promotions. Specialists produce videos. They develop and present webinars and other online programs.

In some situations, PR professionals examine and review a client's operations, raising questions and making marketing suggestions. Specialists with strong verbal skills sometimes

Press kits prepared by PR professionals contain assorted informational materials useful to reporters. Slick, color brochures and video CDs are included in these auto sales packs.

make public speeches and presentations on behalf of clients. They provide media and public tours of client facilities.

PUBLIC RELATIONS MANAGERS AND SPECIALISTS

Professionals in this field keep up a positive public image for their employers. They develop material for release to print, broadcast, and online media.

Public relations managers study the markets in which their clients are involved. They help their employers identify and

Interesting data and product or service descriptions are provided in formats for print, Internet, and TV/radio journalists. Some PR workers specialize in one medium; others are involved in all.

focus on the most promising consumer groups. They plan PR campaigns that will appeal to a target audience. These PR programs may involve a variety of communication tools. Managers also plan and oversee company events. In most situations, they work closely with marketing and advertising staff.

Managers edit and approve press materials produced by their staff. They sometimes write press releases themselves. They make sure all information released to the public is accurate and will not lead to controversies or legal problems. Additionally, they supervise or help produce employee newsletters and other internal relations projects.

When reporters want information or comments from a company or institution, the first point of contact in most cases is the PR office—usually a particular representative. Public relations officers develop working relationships with reporters and editors. They may be able to answer questions and provide background information immediately. If not, they either obtain the information or put the inquirer in direct contact with an appropriate source inside the company.

PR managers or specialists set up press interviews for company executives. They often sit in on interviews and press conferences, available to quickly research and answer detailed questions. Some information specialists draft speeches for their employers and help them communicate effectively.

Public relations specialists are sometimes called "media specialists" or "communications specialists." In government offices, they may have the title "press secretary." For the most part, they handle the writing and other PR development tasks under the direction of managers.

Large agencies may assign certain specialists the primary task of researching and writing press releases. In some workplaces, one PR professional is assigned to develop all the public relations material for one or more clients. The work may

CONNECTING WITH THE COMMUNITY

Aïda Rogers went a long way around the career track before returning to her hometown and joining its public relations efforts. With a degree in journalism and mass communications, she reported education and entertainment for two small city newspapers. She then became a producer and interviewer for a daily television feature program. From there, she entered magazine journalism, becoming the editor of a regional quarterly.

Rogers now serves as visitors and information coordinator at the Greater Lexington Chamber and Visitors Center in South Carolina. It's one of the fastest-growing communities in the Southeast.

"A lot of random things go on," she reports. "People phone and walk in with all sorts of questions. They assume we have information on everything."

Besides major annual events—an oyster roast, wine tasting, golf tournaments, and business exposition—the chamber sponsors as many as three ribbon-cutting ceremonies a week to launch new businesses. Rogers writes and distributes press releases, feature articles, and copy for the town's visitor information packet. She develops Web site content and writes information for the chamber's weekly electronic newsletter. She also participates on the chamber's weekly radio show.

"I really am using my education and experience in a different kind of way," she says. "It's very much a people job. It's very busy, and there's always a surprise."

include writing press releases, producing regular newsletters, providing fresh content for the client's Web site, researching and writing whitepapers, and more.

Specialists trained in public relations usually spearhead the fund-raising projects of nonprofit organizations, finding donors. Some are experienced grant writers.

RELATED JOBS

In some PR firms and departments, employees with specific training and experience are assigned tasks suited to their strengths. Some of the particular specialties include these:

WRITERS AND AUTHORS

Talented writers research and write promotional materials for clients. These range from short, catchy advertising blurbs to articles for company newsletters and magazines. Some writers develop in-depth booklets called whitepapers—and occasionally even book-length documents. Others write scripts for radio, television, and online productions.

TECHNICAL WRITERS

Instruction manuals and other support materials are usually turned over to writers with special technical knowledge. They are able to explain complicated technical concepts and details to their employers and customers.

EDITORS

Editors oversee the preparation and production of print, broadcast, and online promotional materials. They verify accuracy and make revisions as needed.

Using a variety of communication tools, PR professionals are kept busy. Viewing duplicate computer files, they can discuss projects with associates and clients in distant locations.

ARTISTS AND ANIMATORS

These professionals create images and animation for visual promotions. Their work may appear in television commercials, online videos, and documentaries.

PRODUCERS AND DIRECTORS

Producers are in charge of the overall production of video and TV presentations. Projects may also include documentaries, films, and live performances. Directors guide the project step by step. Generally, producers and directors are responsible for turning the work of a scriptwriter into an informative or entertaining presentation.

A CHALLENGING AND GROWING CAREER FIELD

Most PR professionals work full-time. Like those in marketing and advertising, they sometimes work late hours and weekends. They frequently juggle several projects simultaneously. Multiple deadlines contribute to an often stressful environment.

Most of the work is done inside the PR firm or department. Employees also attend interviews, press conferences, and meetings. They attend events within the community and sometimes travel.

The need for PR professionals is growing. The U.S. Bureau of Labor Statistics expects the job market for specialists to grow by 23 percent during the second decade of the century. That would be faster than the national job growth average. It means competition will be very active for college graduates entering the field.

The growth rate for PR management jobs is projected at 16 percent, roughly the average of all occupations.

chapter 3

PREPARING YOURSELF

Marketing and public relations are rooted in communication. Professionals in these careers must be able to communicate effectively with the public and with their employers. They have to be able to clearly convey what their clients sell or offer as a service, why those products would be a good buy, and what's special about the companies they work for.

Most professionals in this field are college graduates with majors in journalism or mass communications, with concentrations in marketing, public relations, or advertising. Some enter the field with degrees in business studies.

Before they decide on a college major, though, young people should make sure they are cut out for PR or marketing as their life's work. They should candidly evaluate their personal traits and serious interests. Certain characteristics are essential.

PERSONAL QUALITIES

Practically all workers in this area must have excellent personal communication skills. They must be able to connect pleasantly with the public and press. Good grammar is a must, since most jobs involve writing, either for the media or for internal publications and reports. For modern communications work, it's assumed they're familiar with computers and know how to find their way around the Internet.

A video editor studies a project on a wide-screen display. Marketing and PR specialists are expected to be focused self-starters who can also collaborate effectively with a team.

Communications specialists must be self-starters who can work unruffled under time pressure. They need to be well organized and possess excellent time management skills. In most settings, they must be good team players. They should be detail-oriented and eager problem solvers. Judgment skills are needed to explain complex and sensitive topics effectively.

Management jobs call for special strengths in decision making, time and money management, motivation, and creative thinking. Managers need to analyze and understand consumer habits and buying trends. They must work effectively with clients who may have very different personalities. They must also be able to inspire their staff to do their best.

EDUCATION AND EXPERIENCE

Most marketing, advertising, and promotions managers and specialists have at least a bachelor's degree in a major such as journalism or advertising. Besides communications courses, they may study economics, market research, consumer behavior, business law, finance and accounting, management, math and statistics, communications technology, photography, and visual arts.

PR managers and specialists typically hold bachelor's degrees in journalism, public relations, or mass communications. Some are English or business majors. In addition to studies in their college major programs, they're advised to take such courses as advertising, public affairs, business administration, technical and creative writing, public speaking, and political science.

Graphic designers have degrees in art or design. Art directors usually have at least a bachelor's degree and several years of experience. Technical

A product adviser demonstrates a newly introduced tablet computer to customers in an electronics store. Product demonstrations—in person, on the air, and online—are proven marketing techniques.

support specialists such as Web site developers and maintainers usually need a technical school or college degree.

Management positions call for several years of experience. Some are open only to candidates with master's degrees. Marketing managers typically work in related occupations for one to five years before they apply for management positions. Experience in advertising, marketing, promotion, sales, public relations, and purchasing is useful.

PR specialists need good research, information gathering, interviewing, and writing skills. Public speaking may be part of their work. Depending on their duties, they may also need skills and experience in layout and design. Increasingly, PR jobs call for involvement in creating and maintaining Web sites and blogs. Many specialists produce and distribute electronic newsletters.

Serving an internship while in college will be a plus for obtaining a job. Workers with management ambitions may improve their advancement opportunities by obtaining certification. The Public Relations Society of America and the International Association of Business Communicators offer certification programs.

Sales managers for large companies command salaries almost as high as those of marketing managers. They typically have business-related degrees. Sales agents, who work with marketing staff at some organizations, may need only a high school diploma. Likewise, product demonstrators and promoters usually require only a high school diploma or its equivalent.

Some PR agencies and departments provide a brief period of on-the-job training for new employees. Trainees perform such tasks as clipping and filing newspaper and magazine articles related to the employer's business. They search the Internet for online news and features. Gradually, they take on writing and other assignments.

TYPICAL JOB LISTINGS

In most regions of the United States, a simple Internet search for "marketing jobs" and "public relations jobs" will turn up scores of openings locally or in cities nearby. Employers are usually agencies or large companies with in-house promotional departments. Job searchers can narrow their results with more precise and expanded search terms defining the kinds of jobs they want. Examples: "market representative entry level," "public relations job entertainment," or "social media Web marketing specialist."

Here are examples of job openings found in online searches:

ENTRY-LEVEL ADVERTISING, MARKETING, SALES, AND PR REPS

An agency representing local and national clients in the sports and entertainment industries has multiple openings. It seeks "competitive" applicants with an "entrepreneurial spirit and winning attitude." Entry-level account representatives are trained on the job to create and manage marketing and ad campaigns. They make presentations and work with clients face to face. Those with special leadership abilities are groomed to manage one of the agency's branch offices. Candidates "must be great with people." Marketing, PR, and advertising positions call for a bachelor's degree. Sales jobs generally do not.

MARKETING COORDINATOR

A manufacturing corporation needs a professional to "support the roll-out of marketing programs to drive sales and to support the marketing communication tactics." Marketing efforts support product launches as well as bundling and up-selling strategies. The coordinator, working under the supervision of

Professionals in a creative office discuss project details. Managers and coordinators oversee and track the status and results of current and completed assignments.

the marketing manager, will track program success, make monthly reports, and recommend "adjustments for optimizing return on investment." Additional duties include writing a weekly marketing report, writing press releases, and maintaining the company Web site. The coordinator must be proficient in Microsoft Office Suite programs and stay informed of "new e-tools and communication platforms." The job requires a bachelor's degree, preferably in marketing or business, and one to three years of marketing experience, "preferably with a national brand."

SENIOR PR ACCOUNT EXECUTIVE

An international communications agency has an opening for a senior account executive to "manage, maintain, and grow relationships" with clients. Clients include major technology companies. The account executive will develop "comprehensive communication plans that clarify business goals, situation analysis, challenges, solutions and measurement." The professional also needs a strong background in "crisis communications." Interestingly, the firm wants someone with the particular ability to "tell stories and form solid partnerships with clients." The job requires a degree in communications, journalism, public policy, or a related major. The successful candidate will have at least four years of PR experience with an agency or corporation and at least one year of experience in team management.

PUBLIC RELATIONS DIRECTOR

A communications firm needs a senior-level executive to direct and expand its PR department. Besides managing and coaching PR staff, the director will work with other firm leaders to create public relations strategies and monitor budgets. The

Project directors train, coach, and lead the staff. They work with other directors and supervisors to plan strategies, establish budgets, and monitor progress.

director must be a veteran in establishing relationships with members of the press. The individual will guide staff in generating positive publicity for clients by pitching stories to the media. A strong understanding of social media is important because social media initiatives are increasingly key parts of PR campaigns. Applicants must have a bachelor's degree in communications, journalism, English, or another PR-related major. At least ten years of PR experience is expected, preferably at an agency.

RÉSUMÉS AND INTERVIEWS

Once you have acquired the necessary education, two things are important for landing a good job: an effective résumé and interviewing confidence.

A résumé is your career self-portrait. It summarizes your talents and skills,

Jonathan Kingsley
2002 Sky Avenue
Warburton, MO 65000
Home: (007) 543-2345; Mobile: (007) 654-3456
tzkingsley@sub90a1.com

Immediate Objective: To obtain a part-time or volunteer position with a marketing or public relations firm that will help me prepare for a lifelong career.

Long-Term Objective: A career as a marketing or public relations specialist and, eventually, manager.

Education

Northside High School (Warburton), Class of 2014 (3.3 GPA).

Work Experience

2012–Present
Part-time stocking assistant, MidCoSave supermarket chain, Warburton.

School Year 2013–2014
Ad sales representative for *Northside Warrior* student newspaper.

2013–Present
Author and promoter of two music-related blogs.

Special Skills and Knowledge

Five years of experience with Windows and Mac desktop and laptop PCs, Android smartphone and tablet devices, standard productivity software, hundreds of mobile apps, and popular social networks.

Elective courses in Web page design and CAD.

Three years of French language studies.

Activities

Writing, laying out, printing, and distributing flyers and other promotional material for four local bands.

Helping staff the phone banks for two local charity fund-raising broadcast campaigns.

References

Marybeth Jones, English teacher, Northside High School; phone (007) 543-7645.

Lawrence Ellis, manager, MidCoSave supermarket, Warburton; phone (007) 543-4637.

This example of a résumé for a part-time or volunteer position with a marketing or PR firm clearly lists the applicant's experience and skills.

education and training, and job experience. It concludes with a list of references—former employers or teachers who will vouch for the quality of your work.

Many people maintain two versions of their résumés. A short, one-page résumé might be simply an introduction of yourself. You will want a detailed profile to submit when applying for an advanced position, where the job competition may be intense.

You should start a résumé while still in high school. Even if you have no work experience, you can state your career objective and begin recording appropriate courses you are taking and skills you are learning. You can note your involvement in school clubs, volunteer activities, and awards or certificates of appreciation for your contributions. You will be updating your résumé often during your career as you acquire new credentials.

You should also think about the job interview process. Most marketing and public relations careers require bachelor's degrees, so it's natural to assume that you will not be seriously interviewing for a job until your senior year in college. Consider, though, that any jobs you can obtain while in school and college will be valuable additions to your résumé. This is true even if the jobs have nothing to do with marketing and PR. It's never too early to begin preparing yourself to be a successful interview candidate.

BE OPEN TO CHANGES

Society is changing, particularly in the realm of electronic communications. Businesses, industries, and organizations expand, merge, and scale back. Meanwhile, marketing and PR firms regularly change in structure, staff, and specialty areas. Managers and staff acquire new interests and see new opportunities. The job you find right out of college may be very different from the one you have twenty years later.

Some of today's marketing and PR leaders have backed into their careers. Amy Juers at Edge Legal Marketing obtained her undergraduate degree in business. Her initial plan was to find a career in corporate wellness. "I was an aerobics instructor and into healthy eating," she reflects, "and wanted to turn that into a career." Her first job out of college was with a company that helped corporations promote health and well-being for their employees.

She entered graduate school, focusing on business studies but with an emphasis on information systems. That led to a job with a litigation support company. Litigation support involves managing massive volumes of information for lawyers as they prepare cases for trial. Juers became the company's business analyst and marketing manager. That, she says, "was the beginning stage of my marketing and PR career."

chapter 4

WORKING FREELANCE

Would you like to be your own boss? Independent-minded writers, editors, artists, designers, and others involved in marketing and public relations are finding opportunities to establish freelance careers. Computers and the Internet make it easier than ever before to work from anywhere.

Typically, freelancers in this field begin by working for marketing, PR, or advertising agencies or corporate marketing departments. On the side, they might take on small assignments for clients not directly competing with the work of their employer firms. Eventually, they see opportunities to work independently on promotional projects for clients not represented by any marketing agency. Or they might set themselves up as independent specialists and perform contractual work for different agencies.

Most freelancers work in offices or office nooks that they have created at home. A few lease small commercial office space, preferring to strictly separate their work and home life.

Freelance possibilities are available especially to those experienced in public relations. In effect, freelance ("contract") workers can establish solo PR firms. The BLS's *Occupational Outlook Handbook* reports, "Employment is likely to grow in public relations firms as organizations contract out public relations services rather than support more full-time staff when additional work is needed."

Freelancers create their own workspace at home. They can dress casually, set their own schedules, and choose clients and tasks that fit their interests and skills.

Marketing agencies and corporations are increasingly interested in hiring literary and artistic talent from outside the office for onetime projects. This means the agencies don't have to cover employee benefits such as health plans and insurance.

FREELANCE ADVANTAGES AND DISADVANTAGES

The dream of many young marketing and PR professionals is to establish their own businesses. Before they do, they need to understand the financial, insurance, legal, and other business requirements.

Working for themselves as private contractors, freelancers do not receive health, retirement, or other job benefits. They must buy their own insurance and set up their own retirement accounts. They pay for their office equipment, furniture, and utility services. They have to keep careful income and expense records and make proper tax filings and payments. Depending on city zoning regulations, they might not be allowed to operate a business from a residence. If they are allowed, they may be required to obtain business licenses and pay fees.

After looking into it closely, many individuals decide they don't really want to own a business.

However, handsome per-hour and per-project fees can offset the lack of benefits. Freelancers certainly enjoy greater career freedom. Once established, they can become choosy in selecting the projects that interest them most. They set their own work schedules. (However, many of them work longer hours for themselves than agency or department personnel work for companies that hire them.)

A VARIETY OF FREELANCE OPPORTUNITIES

Good writing is a talent that is much in demand in the marketing world. Freelancers can obtain work by writing press releases for local organizations and businesses. They may be contracted by corporate communications managers to write and/or edit newsletters, internal magazines, annual reports, and other publications. Some writers have found lucrative assignments writing newspaper or magazine feature articles for business clients. Others are paid to research and write regular articles for commercial bloggers.

This design professional uses a combination of touchscreen and keyboard technology in his work. Freelancers are responsible for buying their own equipment and managing their businesses.

Many graphic designers also freelance. They are hired to perform projects for agencies whose regular art staffs are too busy. Some work directly for business clients.

Freelancers with both writing and design skills might establish desktop publishing services. They create flyers and materials for mass mailings. They can also produce lengthier materials, such as newsletters.

There are freelance opportunities for Web development specialists and others with technical skills. Some work on contract or retainer for multiple client agencies and organizations.

Perhaps a less likely freelance prospect for those exploring a marketing career is telemarketing. Telephone solicitation is not for thin-skinned individuals. Callers frequently encounter rude receptions. Some telemarketers, though, serve in roles that are unquestionably noble. Employers include charity organizations that depend on fund-raising.

Others are goodwill organizations that hire callers to solicit used clothing and furniture.

Many telemarketers are hired to work from home. They can put in as much or as little time as they wish and set flexible hours.

Telemarketers usually do not need a high school diploma, but they must be able to communicate clearly and pleasantly by phone. No experience is required. After a brief training period, they are put to work. Most earn modest wages and work only until they can obtain more promising employment. The customer-level interaction they experience, however, gives them valuable insight into the world of marketing.

GHOSTWRITING

One way that companies and products become well known is for their founders and managers to become widely recognized. A select few engineers, architects, technology developers, lawyers, and others establish themselves as leaders in their professions. They become locally and even nationally famous when their bylined articles regularly appear in print and they speak at conferences, workshops, and public events.

Interestingly, some of these experts whose bylines become prominent are not good writers. They don't like to write, have little time for it, and rarely attempt to write for publication. They pay ghostwriters to do their writing for them.

It's a partnership. The expert provides the knowledge. The ghostwriter organizes the information and expresses it in an interesting, easy-to-understand way. Ghostwriters aren't bothered that their articles are published with someone else' name attached. Most are paid well for their work. Some write long whitepapers and even books.

Trade journals in different industries constantly seek well-written pieces by insiders in their fields. So do mainstream

BAD PR MAKES BAD IMPRESSIONS

The most successful writers of press releases and commercial features understand that the stories they submit to the media must be truly newsworthy. Each article must provide fresh, useful information about their clients or their clients' products and services.

Too often, media reporters and editors receive press releases and articles that are poorly written. Many contain no new information, merely a rehash of a client's familiar marketing spin. Some releases are obviously drawn from advertising copy—often word for word. It's obvious at a glance that the item would be of little interest to newspaper readers or television viewers. Predictably, it goes into the trash.

A marketing or PR representative who consistently provides legitimate news earns the respect of editors. One who cranks out advertising fluff and presents it as news earns scorn and rarely finds an audience.

magazines and newspapers. A marketing or PR firm or freelancer is the go-between.

The media specialist contacts an editor and pitches an article idea, outlining what the story will be about and how long it will be. If the editor likes the idea, the PR supplier is given a go-ahead to submit the piece on speculation. That means the editor does not promise to actually publish it until the document is completed and approved.

Usually, the ghostwriter involved in the project researches the subject and then interviews the expert "author" in person or by phone or e-mail. The ghostwriter then shapes the article, drawing from statements made by the expert, product descriptions, and research notes. The expert reviews the first draft of the article. The expert might make corrections and clarifications or suggest that certain passages be deleted or expanded. After the article is fine-tuned to the expert's satisfaction, it is submitted to the periodical editor.

Some marketing and PR firms assign writing specialists on their staff to collaborate with clients in ghostwriting projects. Others contract with freelance writers who specialize in ghostwriting.

The best ghostwriters study their subjects carefully. They listen closely to interview recordings to learn the client's style of expression. They try to put themselves inside the minds of their clients and communicate using terms, phrases, and examples that their employers often use in person.

TIP FOR SUCCESS: SPECIALIZE

Amy Juers at Edge Legal Marketing offers a bit of wisdom for a young person embarking on a marketing or public relations career: "Pick a path and become an expert."

Specialties abound. Individuals with writing talents might focus on press releases or ad and promotional copywriting. You might sell your services as a publicist. If you're especially intrigued by the Internet and its potential as an avenue for marketing and PR, you can become a social media marketer or an expert at search engine optimization (SEO).

"But don't try them all," Juers emphasizes. "The world is moving much too fast to be a jack of all trades. Just master one."

chapter 5

CONNECTING WITH CLIENTS

The mission of marketing and public relations firms is to promote their clients. To obtain clients, they have to promote themselves. They often use some of the same methods to promote their own services as they use to promote clients.

Branding is an example. Amy Juers, president of Edge Legal Marketing in St. Paul, Minnesota, recounts that the agency initially was named LegalVoice. They decided to rebrand it in 2007. Since then, the primary methods of getting new clients have shifted. "A lot of leads were generated through e-mail campaigns and attending industry shows and events and meeting people," Juers says. "By 2013, a lot of new growth was based on referrals. We have a lot of strong relationships that seem to carry us forward."

Elaine Gillespie at the Gillespie Agency in Columbia, South Carolina, has represented an astonishing variety of clients. They have included a noted rock musician, banking institutions, restaurant chains, a professional wrestling superstar, an animal adoption agency, a factory outlet store, a public utility company, a mobile network company, a private school, and a brick-making company.

How did she build her agency into the diverse, prominent marketing firm that it is today?

Gillespie's response: "John Lennon once said, 'Life is what happens to you while you're busy making other plans.' That's

The company's famous bitten fruit makes it obvious that this is an Apple, Inc., store, located in New York City. The image is an unmistakable component of the corporate brand.

sort of what happened to the Gillespie Agency. While we were busy working and making our clients happy, others were taking notice. I spent the first ten years pitching new accounts and cold calling. Then, almost overnight, companies started calling me."

BUSINESS-BUILDING STRATEGIES

In a nutshell, the way to build a successful marketing or PR business is to do good work. To achieve that, professionals begin by thoroughly familiarizing themselves with what the client offers. They determine which marketing and PR strategies will work best for a particular client. They plan their time and expenditures carefully to ensure that the client receives the best possible return on investment (ROI).

Established marketing professionals point out several strategies for client growth. Firms should consistently deliver high-quality promotional efforts that generate marked results. They should exhibit a can-do attitude. And they should constantly look for new ways to promote their clients.

Gillespie emphasizes the long-term value of consistently performing quality work. "Good clients build relationships with good agencies. If your reputation precedes you, clients will want to work with you. It's important to always deliver more than 100 percent. You will get credit for today's good results a few years in the future."

Also essential is an enthusiastic attitude. As an example, she recalls a potential new client once asking her if she could get his product on TV game shows as one of the prizes. The publicity, he knew, would be more than worth the cost of the giveaways. Gillespie told him frankly that she didn't know how to go about it.

Valuable prizes appeal to contestants and viewers alike in TV game shows. The companies that donate the prizes get publicity that is far more valuable than the items they give away.

"It was Friday afternoon. I went home and thought all weekend about letting the client down. On Monday, I called and said, 'I can get you on game shows!' Of course, I had no idea how I would accomplish it."

His response was astonishing. "Good," he said. "Here's the agent you need to call." He already had the contact information that would make her task easy. He simply was looking for a PR representative who could inspire confidence. The new

MEETING CLIENT NEEDS

Elaine Gillespie is an artist. She obtained a bachelor's degree in studio art. After college graduation, she floundered in graphic art jobs that little interested her. Frustrated, she says, "I went to the largest agency in town and asked if I could work for free. I said, 'The deal is that if you like my work after two weeks, you have to hire me. If you don't, well, you get two weeks of free labor.'"

They liked her work. After four years with the agency, she felt confident to go freelance. Her new agency's offerings rapidly expanded from graphic design to full-service marketing and PR.

"There was no real business plan to become a full-service agency," Gillespie says. "It was simply gaining experience and meeting client needs. If they needed a copywriter, I found one. If they needed a media plan, I learned how to create one. Oh—you want a press conference? I can do that! Eventually, I realized that I could provide much more to my clients than a graphic designer."

Gillespie reflects, "I used to say that we were best known for print design and production efficiencies. But because of the changing times and bringing some strong talent in-house, we are pretty well known for getting publicity for our clients these days— publicity in the arena of media coverage, events, and social media."

client became one of Gillespie's most profitable long-term accounts.

Juers at Edge Legal Marketing cites an important strategy for attracting new clients: offering new services. "You always need to keep innovating and creating," she says, "or you'll risk dying on the vine." The Internet has given marketers broader capabilities to expand their services.

High-profile sponsorships are a proven marketing tactic. Sponsors of race car teams, for example, get constant exposure before thousands of spectators as well as television audiences.

SERVING A MARKET NICHE

Juers says her firm enjoys a valuable advantage because it serves a niche category of clients: law firms and vendors of products for lawyers. "Law firms and legal vendors often turn to us because of our knowledge and expertise specifically in this industry. Unlike other agencies, Edge can hit the ground running because we understand 'legal' and our clients typically do not need to educate us on who they are or what they offer to clients."

Numerous marketing and PR firms work exclusively with music or sports celebrity clients. Most focus on a particular genre or sport. For example, an agency that represents recording artists is likely to concentrate on country, rock, alternative, blues, etc. It establishes key contacts with print, broadcast, and online media in the chosen area. Its agents have an intimate understanding of the specific music audience.

Promoting celebrities might seem glamorous. Work in the performing and visual arts, though, is not a matter of hobnobbing daily with musicians, actors, and artists. It can be especially demanding because famous people have high expectations of their agents.

Other niche markets include professional clients (law firms, accountants, or tax professionals, for example). Certain agencies specialize in the high-tech industry, promoting computer- and Internet-related products and services. Some firms function as publicists for authors. Some work for publishing houses, theatrical companies, lecturers, and consultants.

Large marketing and publicity firms might handle scores or even hundreds of client accounts. Other firms concentrate their efforts on representing only a handful of major clients.

WORD OF MOUTH GROWS THE BUSINESS

Building a solid reputation is all-important. Many new clients come through referrals from old clients.

Gillespie once received a call from a lawyer for whom she had done publicity work. One of his legal clients needed similar help, and the lawyer believed Gillespie was perfect for the task. He arranged an appointment.

The mystery legal client turned out to be a sixteen-time world championship wrestler. He was planning to retire from the ring and wanted to start a business that would take advantage of his stardom.

"We sat at the conference table and discussed Web sites and marketing for about an hour," she relates. "Then he said, 'Would you be my agent?'"

Gillespie had never promoted a sports celebrity. She told him she wasn't sure how to go about it. He persisted, and she eventually agreed to represent him.

"What a learning experience that was! But we jumped right in and booked him for hundreds of appearances over the next three years. This was a strange extension of advertising and public relations, but somehow it all worked hand in hand."

chapter 6

AVENUES OF COMMUNICATION

Successful marketing is basically a two-part process. Creating good publicity material and presentations is the first part of the job. The second is getting the public's attention. Even the most creative, powerful marketing campaigns are worthless without an audience.

That calls for establishing effective working relationships with the media. Media channels deliver the message to the masses.

Spot advertising requires little contact between an advertising representative and the media or public. It's purely a business transaction: buying ad space in a periodical, commercial time on radio or television, or Internet ad placement. Mass-circulation advertising and promotional activities are also cut-and-dried. They involve compiling a list of postal mail or e-mail addresses and distributing the material. Telemarketers, meanwhile, make cold calls to strangers. Their success relies on their powers of persuasion over the phone, one customer at a time.

Newer forms of publicity go beyond the basic selling process. They have long-term objectives. They are based on building relationships between marketing or PR specialists and members of the media. Successful relationships are nurtured over a period of months and years.

Telephone operators are hired to process donor calls in fund-raising promotions and make cold calls in telemarketing campaigns. Career marketing workers can gain valuable experience staffing phone banks.

MARKETING THEN AND NOW

In the beginning, marketing consisted simply of advertising. The first advertising agency in the United States was started in 1842. Advertising was done mainly through newspapers, posters, and catalogs. For many years to come, advertisers tried to entice customers with fantastic promises. In most instances, the people who created the ads knew little or nothing about the products they were advertising. Their questionable and sometimes completely false claims were exposed. Customers were angered. The advertising business got a bad reputation that it has never completely lived down.

Merchants and their agents began to understand that shrewd buyers were impressed more by facts than exaggerations. They realized there were indirect ways to increase sales. If they could build up the company's image, it would create public interest—and trust—in the company's products.

This new "public relations" strategy was carried out not through advertisements but by making the company newsworthy. Promoters looked for opportunities to have their clients favorably discussed, or at least mentioned, in news articles. Readers then saw the companies not merely as sellers but as reliable sources of information. It was free, positive publicity.

THE PITCH

Modern marketers and publicists have perfected a sophisticated technique to create a lasting public image. They promote clients by molding them into experts. Marketing professionals "pitch" their clients to the media. They make clients available for interviews to discuss current events and issues. But they don't wait for reporters to come to them. They repeatedly present their clients as sources of worthwhile information.

One way to do that is to arrange for the publication of articles and research studies written by the client. PR specialists approach newspaper, magazine, and newsletter editors to pitch article ideas. If an idea sounds interesting, editors are usually receptive. They are being offered an exclusive piece written by a knowledgeable industry insider (or an approved ghostwriter). Better still, they don't have to pay for it. The PR agency covers the time and any expense required to produce the material.

If an editor shows an interest, the PR professional must make sure the project is done well. A good article will make it easier to pitch others in the future. A bad one can make it harder to get a foot in the editor's door next time.

Getting a foot in the door the first time is largely a matter of introducing yourself to the right media people. Amy Juers at Edge Legal Marketing says, "Just like no two businesses are alike, no two reporters or editors and their publications are alike. The challenge is to find your way in, find the right contacts, and continue to build and maintain relationships."

A marketing professional uses a flipchart to illustrate a presentation. Marketing and public relations tasks often include speaking engagements and product demonstrations.

RELATIONS, NOT TRANSACTIONS

While nurturing their media connections, marketers and their clients today are building webs of relationships directly with consumers. In times past, marketing tactics ended at the point of sale (the transaction). Now the sale hopefully is only the beginning of a long-term relationship that will lead to more sales. Social networks provide the communications avenue that makes "relationship marketing" possible.

Mari Smith, a social media marketing consultant and author of *The New Relationship Marketing*, has posted a list of "best practices" for relationship-based marketing on her blog. She observes, "With the vast range of social media tools at our disposal today, it's easier now more than ever to shift your focus from transactional marketing to relationship marketing. Your customers and prospects want to know that you're listening, that they are important to you, and that you are striving to improve your brand, products and services as a result of their feedback. You can't afford to be a one-way broadcast channel."

Technology is the tool that enables a two-way relationship between sellers and buyers. But marketers should focus on the relationships, not the medium. The successful relationship marketer, Smith says, "embraces high-tech but always maintains high-touch by constantly reaching out to the public."

She adds, "For editors and reporters that we have very strong relationships with, the proposal and pitching process is streamlined and routine. After you get to know these people, you learn what they like and what they expect. You can become a very good resource for them."

WORKING IN A DIGITAL WORLD

In the early years, almost all marketing, advertising, and public relations was done through print media: newspapers, mail-order catalogs, posters, and signs. Broadcast media—first radio, then television—brought marketers new ways to reach consumers. Still, print marketing remained vital.

The digital age is changing that. Already, marketing campaigns involve Web sites, e-mail, social media, blogs, live chats, and other online media. People are spending less time reading printed newspapers and magazines and more time getting information online. Futurists predict the next generation will hardly use printed matter at all.

That does not mean marketing and public relations are dying career fields. They are more thriving—and exciting—than ever before. Professionals entering this job market will simply be doing more of their work digitally instead of in print. They will find new ways to use the Internet to promote products and services.

Competition is expected to be stiff. Those who have the greatest digital skills and understanding will have the inside track on the best jobs.

A SECURE FUTURE

The *Occupational Outlook Handbook* notes, "Advertising, promotions, and marketing will continue to be essential for organizations as they look to maintain and expand their share of the market." It adds, "Because marketing managers and their departments are important to an organization's revenue, marketing managers are less likely to be let go than other types of managers. Marketing managers will continue to be in demand as organizations seek to market their product to specific customers and localities."

Increasingly, marketing and sales efforts are directed toward online shoppers. Even consumers who prefer to buy in stores frequently compare products on the Internet before making their decisions.

In his book *Ad Land*, which traces the history of advertising and marketing, author Mark Tungate draws an interesting conclusion. "What makes advertising so fascinating right now," he says, "is that nobody really knows how it will evolve."

Already, social media such as blogs, Facebook, and Twitter are changing the way that marketing and PR programs are carried out. The *Occupational Outlook Handbook* predicts the increasing use of social media is especially promising for people interested in PR careers. "These new media outlets will create more work for public relations workers, increasing the number and kinds of avenues of communication between organizations and the public. Public relations specialists will be needed to help clients use these new types of media effectively."

Whatever the medium, marketing and public relations professionals will remain vital, if sellers are to communicate effectively with buyers. Specialists are needed to convince consumers that products are worth the money and their suppliers can be trusted.

glossary

account A business arrangement between a marketing or PR firm and a client.

blog A Web log; a personal journal published on the World Wide Web.

bundling Offering a combination of products or services for a bargain price.

byline The name of a writer as it appears with a published article or book.

client An individual, business, or organization employing a marketing or PR firm.

commercial Pertaining to a retail business; for example, commercial office space.

consumer A buyer and user of products or services.

contractual work The work performed by an independent agent or agency under terms of a short- or long-term contract, rather than by a regular employee.

digital Having to do with numbers, commonly used in reference to electronic information.

enterprise A business operation.

free enterprise The freedom of private businesses to function without excessive interference from the government.

investor One who provides financial backing to a business in hopes of earning a profit share.

media Plural of medium; the people who work in the communications business.

medium Newspaper, television, or another channel of communications.

pitch To suggest an article idea to the editor of a periodical.

retainer The fee that a client pays a marketer or other professional to be available to perform services when needed.

return on investment (ROI) The amount of profit a client realizes from a marketing campaign or other business investment.

search engine optimization (SEO) Making a Web page one of the first to be listed in search engine results.

up-selling Suggesting an additional or more expensive product when a consumer places an order.

webinar A seminar or training session conducted via the Internet.

whitepaper A lengthy, in-depth article or research paper.

for more information

American Association of Advertising Agencies (4A's)
1065 Avenue of the Americas, 16th Floor
New York, NY 10018
(212) 682-2500
Web site: http://www.aaaa.org
This association counsels member agencies, fosters professional development, and encourages high creative and
business standards.

Canadian Marketing Association (CMA)
1 Concorde Gate, Suite 607
Don Mills, ON M3C 3N6
Canada
(416) 391-2362
Web site: https://www.the-cma.org
The CMA develops programs to help members in all market-
ing disciplines, channels, and technologies.

Canadian Public Relations Society (CPRS)
4195 Dundas Street West, Suite 346
Toronto, ON M8X 1Y4
Canada
(416) 239-7034
Web site: http://www.cprs.ca
Members of the CPRS "work to maintain the highest standards and to share a uniquely Canadian experience in
public relations."

Institute for Public Relations
P.O. Box 118400

2096 Weimer Hall
Gainesville, FL 32611-8400
(352) 392-0280
Web site: http://www.instituteforpr.org
An independent, nonprofit foundation, the institute is dedicated to "the science beneath the art of public relations."

International Association of Business Communicators (IABC)
601 Montgomery Street, Suite 1900
San Francisco, CA 94111
(415) 544-4700
Web site: http://www.iabc.com
The IABC is a professional network whose members work in public and media relations, corporate communications, public affairs, investor relations, government relations, marketing communication, community relations, writing, editing, training and teaching, advertising, photography and video production, graphic design, and human resources.

International Public Relations Association (IPRA)
P.O. Box 6945
London, W1A 6US
United Kingdom
+ 44 1903 744442
Web site: http://www.ipra.org
The IPRA, an association of public relations practitioners around the world, promotes the exchange of information and professional development opportunities.

Public Relations Society of America (PRSA)
33 Maiden Lane, 11th Floor
New York, NY 10038-5150
(212) 460-1400

Web site: http://www.prsa.org
The PRSA provides professional development, sets standards of excellence, and upholds ethical principles for public relations workers.

U.S. Bureau of Labor Statistics (BLS)
Division of Information and Marketing Services
2 Massachusetts Avenue NE, Room 2850
Washington, DC 20212
(202) 691-5200
Web site: http://www.bls.gov
An agency within the U.S. Department of Labor, the BLS measures labor market activity, working conditions, and other economic factors concerning the U.S. labor market. Its *Occupational Outlook Handbook* provides career information on hundreds of occupations. (For example, search jobs such as marketing research analysts; advertising, promotions, and marketing managers; public relations managers and specialists; and advertising sales agents.)

WEB SITES

Due to the changing nature of Internet links, Rosen Publishing has developed an online list of Web sites related to the subject of this book. This site is updated regularly. Please use this link to access the list:

http://www.rosenlinks.com/EC/PubRe

for further reading

Ferguson Publishing. *Advertising and Marketing* (Ferguson's Careers in Focus). 2nd ed. New York, NY: Ferguson, 2009.

Ferguson Publishing. *Public Relations* (Ferguson's Careers in Focus). New York, NY: Ferguson, 2007.

Moore, Edward. *School Public Relations for Student Success.* Thousand Oaks, CA: Corwin, 2009.

Newsom, Doug, Judy VanSlyke Turk, and Dean Kruckeberg. *This Is PR: The Realities of Public Relations* (Wadsworth Series in Mass Communication and Journalism). 11th ed. Beverly, MA: Wadsworth Publishing, 2013.

Niver, Heather Moore. *Dream Jobs in Sports Marketing* (Great Careers in the Sports Industry). New York, NY: Rosen Publishing, 2013.

Platform Online Magazine. The Plank Center for Leadership in Public Relations, University of Alabama. Quarterly (http://platformmagazine.org).

PRWeek. Haymarket Media, Inc. Weekly (http://www.prweekus.com).

Salter, Brian. *Successful Public Relations in a Week* (Teach Yourself: Business). New York, NY: McGraw-Hill, 2013.

Sherman, Gerald J., and Sar Perlman. *Fashion Public Relations.* New York, NY: Fairchild Books, 2010.

Stair, Leslie. *Careers in Marketing.* New York, NY: McGraw-Hill, 2008.

Stinson, Paul. *Sales, Marketing, Business, and Finance* (Great Careers with a High School Diploma). New York, NY: Facts On File, 2008.

Tymorek, Stan. *Advertising and Public Relations* (Career Launcher). New York, NY: Checkmark Books, 2010.

Weinick, Suzanne. *Increasing Your Tweets, Likes, and Ratings: Marketing Your Digital Business* (Digital Entrepreneurship in the Age of Apps, the Web, and Mobile Devices). New York, NY: Rosen Publishing, 2012.

bibliography

Field, Shelly. *Career Opportunities in Advertising and Public Relations*. 4th ed. New York, NY: Checkmark Books, 2006.

Gillespie, Elaine. Personal interview. April 2013.

Juers, Amy. Personal interview. March 2013.

Kursmark, Louise. *How to Start a Home-Based Desktop Publishing Business*. Guilford, CT: The Globe Pequot Press, 2002.

Morgan, Jacob. "What Is Social CRM?" *Social Media Examiner*, November 3, 2010. Retrieved April 2013 (http://www.socialmediaexaminer.com/what-is-social-crm).

Rogers, Aïda. Personal interview. April 2013.

Smith, Mari. "12 Tenets of Relationship Marketing Effectiveness." MariSmith.com, October 27, 2011. Retrieved April 2013 (http://www.marismith.com/tenets-of-relationship-marketing-effectiveness).

Sullivan, John. "PR Industry Fills Vacuum Left by Shrinking Newsrooms." *ProPublica*, May 1, 2011. Retrieved April 2013 (http://www.propublica.org/article/pr-industry-fills-vacuum-left-by-shrinking-newsrooms).

Tungate, Mark. *Ad Land: A Global History of Advertising*. London, England, and Philadelphia, PA: Kogan Page Ltd., 2007.

U.S. Department of Labor, Bureau of Labor Statistics. "Advertising, Promotions, and Marketing Managers." *Occupational Outlook Handbook*. Retrieved January 2013 (http://www.bls.gov/ooh/management/advertising-promotions-and-marketing-managers.htm).

U.S. Department of Labor, Bureau of Labor Statistics. "Public Relations Managers and Specialists." *Occupational Outlook Handbook*. Retrieved January 2013 (http://www.bls.gov/

ooh/management/public-relations-managers-and-specialists.htm).

U.S. Department of Labor, Bureau of Labor Statistics. Various sections. *Occupational Outlook Handbook*. Retrieved January 2013 (www.bls.gov/ooh).

Wynne, Robert. "What Does a Public Relations Agency Do?" *Forbes*, April 10, 2013. Retrieved April 2013 (http://www.forbes.com/sites/robertwynne/2013/04/10/what-does-a-public-relations-agency-do).

index

About the Author

Daniel E. Harmon has written more than eighty books and thousands of magazine, newspaper, and newsletter articles. As a periodicals editor, he has sifted through countless marketing and PR submissions ranging in quality from excellent to poor. He has ghostwritten in-depth magazine articles for executives in the technology industry. Harmon has more than fifteen years of experience as a Web site designer, Web and blog content creator, and book publicist.

Photo Credits

Cover (figure) Elena Elisseeva/Shutterstock.com; cover (background), p. 1 Jon Feingersh/Blend Images/Getty Images; p. 4 ImageSource/Getty Images; p. 8 Radius Images/Getty Images; p. 10 Hoang Dinh Nam/AFP/Getty Images; pp. 12–13 Stephen Simpson/Iconica/Getty Images; p. 16 Izabela Habur/the Agency Collection/Getty Images; pp. 20–21, 34–35 © AP Images; pp. 22–23 Chip Somodevilla/Getty Images; p. 25 © Bill Aron/PhotoEdit; p. 26 Julija Sapic/Shutterstock.com; p. 30 Christopher Robbins/Digital Vision/Thinkstock; p. 33 © iStockphoto.com/Chris Schmidt; p. 38 Monkey Business Images/Shutterstock.com; pp. 40–41 auremar/Shutterstock.com; p. 46 Photodisc/Thinkstock; pp. 48–49 Roberto Westbrook/Blend Images /Getty Images; pp. 54–55 Songquan Deng/Shutterstock.com; p. 56 CBS Photo Archive/Getty Images; p. 58 Cal Sport Media/AP Images; p. 62 Pressmaster/Shutterstock.com; p. 64 John Rowley/Digital Vision/Thinkstock; p. 67 © iStockphoto.com/dem10; back cover (background) © iStockphoto .com/blackred.

Designer: Matt Cauli; Editor: Kathy Kuhtz Campbell;
Photo Researcher: Karen Huang